On the Textobject & Its Concealment

CLOAK VI

The object, in its growing autonomy, establishes defense mechanisms to protect itself from outside antagonisms.

^

A vestigial skin (integumentary drapery) — CLOAK

^

The CLOAK is the material witness of your concealment // of your absence. It denotes your position against a system of surveillance.

^

—An interdisciplinary zone, contaminated by the co-mingling of disparate media objects—realized both physically and virtually.

The role of the object is two-fold. First to position itself as something independent of the user (which does not rely on the subject's capacity to interface). And second, to observe / document its environment—looking back as it is looked upon. Articulating a multi-directionality within the acts of READING & VIEWING.

Note: That this is not an ontology oriented towards the object, but rather an expanding of the object's functionality within an egalitarian system. The object does not usurp the subject, rather it grows more complex as a participant of the mediums that are often projected atop it.

Andrew Culp states that "faciality becomes a regime of self-capture" and vies for a tactical form of invisibility.

^

Deleuze and Guattari, in unison: "Why have we kept our own names? Out of habit, purely out of habit. To make ourselves unrecognizable in turn. To render imperceptible, not ourselves, but what makes us act, feel, and think."

^

And thus we find an alternative method to the invisible, not in the immediacy of an optical obfuscation, but in the concealment of the means, the method, the praxis.

It hides what stratagem wait beneath.

˄

In this sense creating a certain subterranean element to the CLOAK's deployment.

˄

Positioning the object's expanded repitoire as something emergent. Its revelation as an unearthing.

˄

Beneath the surface, there is a greater capacity for concealment. It is easier to hide oneself out of the sun's reach.

˄

The CLOAK is an anti-solarist tool. Its creation is distinctly digital. The text is written on a computer. In Word, Google Drive, Notepad. Its shape is arranged on InDesign, PowerPoint, Rhino. Its body is produced by IngramSpark, KDP, BookMobile.

˄

In each step of the process, the object's anatomy is obscured from our view. We are engaging with a surface—with a filtering of what we are allowed to see.

˄

The guts remain out of reach / out of sight.

˄

In revealing the work, we reveal an opening into the earth. An alternative route. A way in.

˄

The surface   the behaviors & methodologies of its interior.

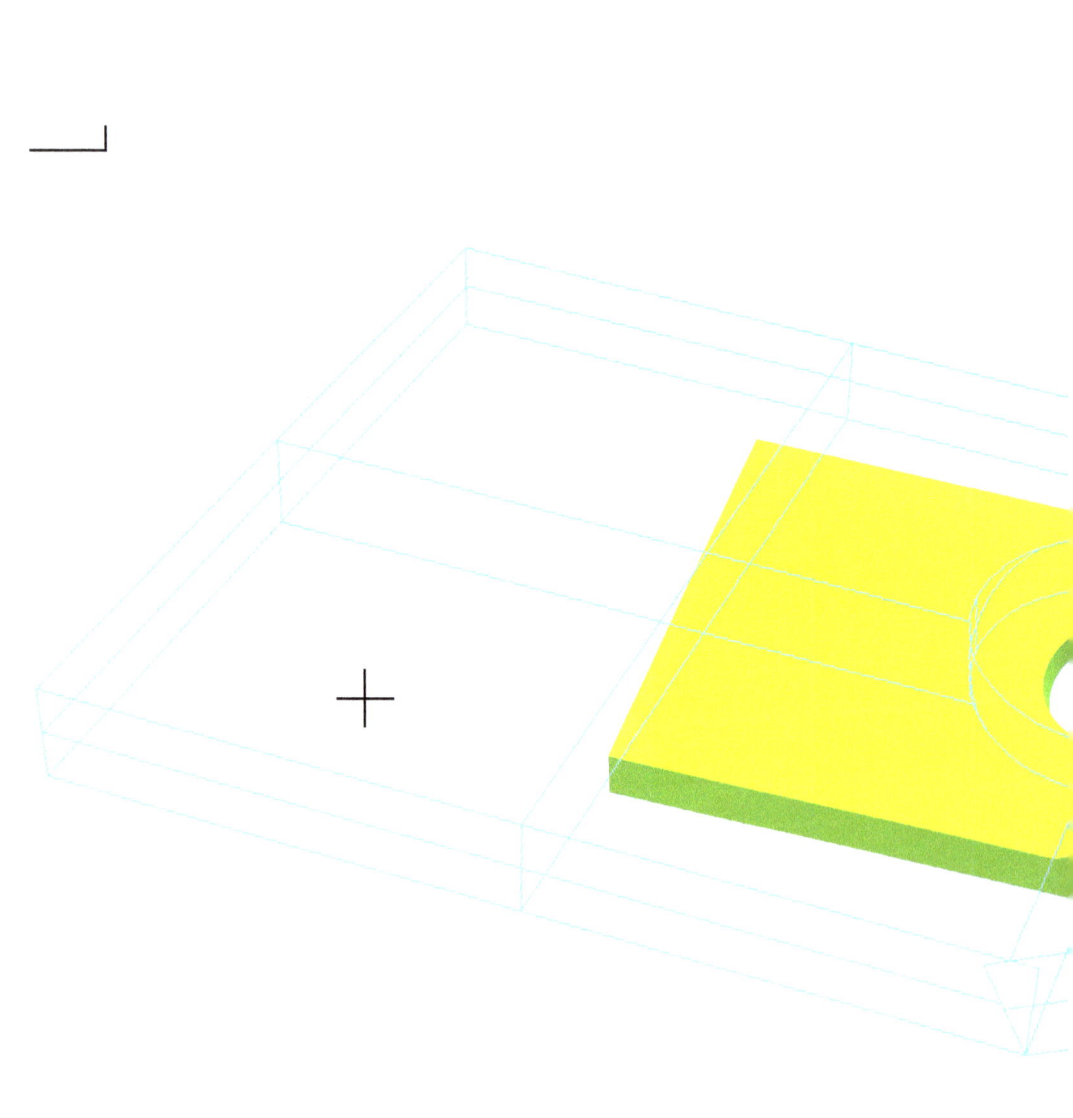

...RECT ROUTE—
...RING THE ORIFICE

MOTIVE: EXT → INT

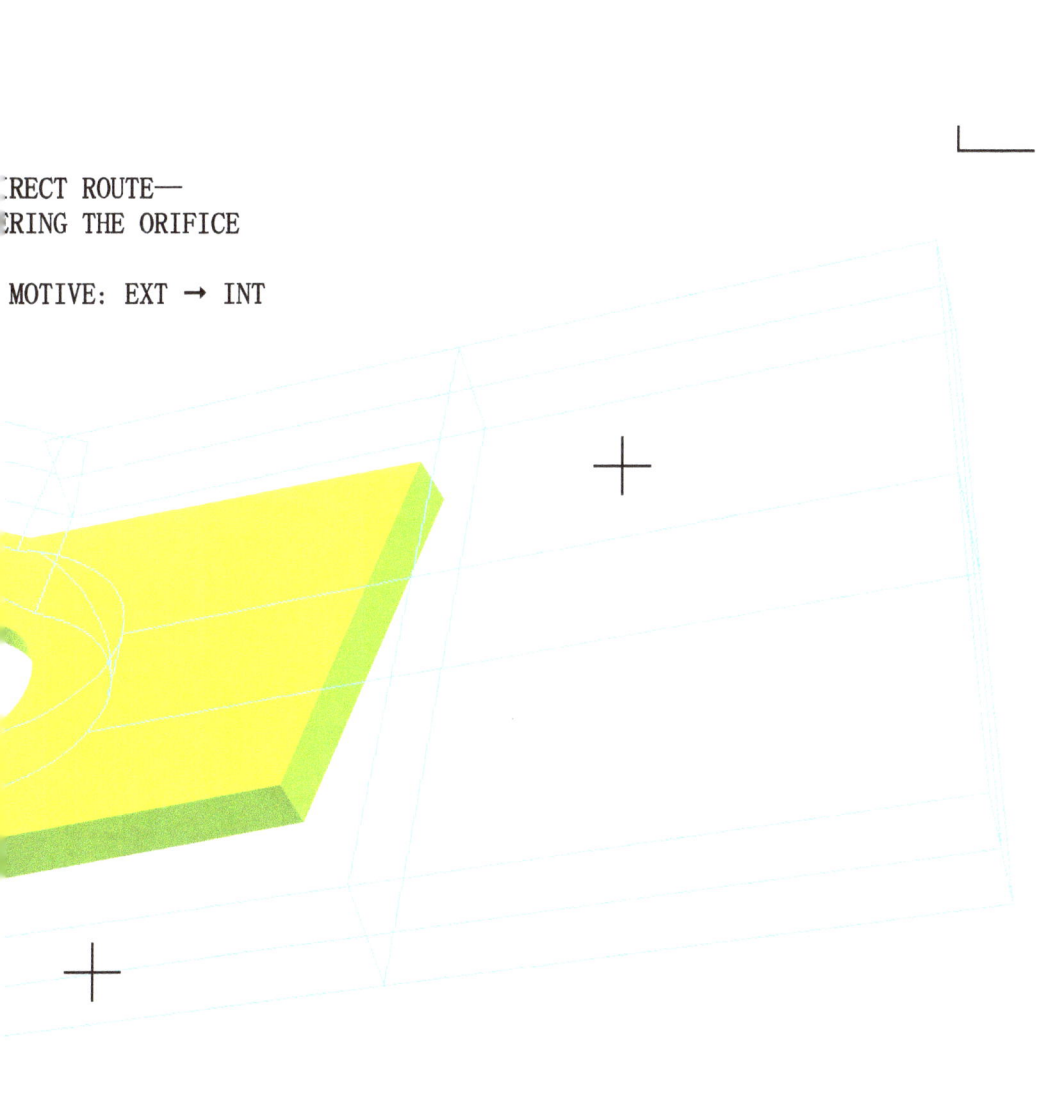

THROUGH THE THRESHOLD BETWEEN INT & EXT
A SET OF LIMBS PROTRUDE

THEY ARE A DISTRACTION
THE OBJECT FLEXES ITS EXPANDED OPTICAL CAPACITY

IS THIS IN COLOR?
ARE WE TERRAFORMING AN ARTIFICAL NODE?

THE OBJECT — TEXTOBJECT — WRITHES

But the _____ does not fully reveal the interior. We still must speculate what exists in these predominantly occulted zones. The unknown chasm of the gutter. Its pull of ___ eye towards a bloated crevice (a field of anuses).

^

I fantasize an opening of the page, slowly reaching inside and finding my hand in a vast atrium—somewhere so large that I cannot feel the edges. The walls or the ceiling. The floor.

^

Out in the open. In in the open (Abyssopelagic void).

^

The CLOAK hides an endless expanse. Where the textobject can chameleon itself as every accompanying medium. Using its intestines as makeshift cilia, prodding at their environment.

^

The invisible interior creates a space in which the textobject can act unobserved, developing these new traits / tools / systems.

^

We are not made invisible by hiding from the ubiquitous eyes of the surveillance system, but through camoflauge and distraction.

^

The textobject appears as if it is a book. The book appears as if it is something only intended to be read.

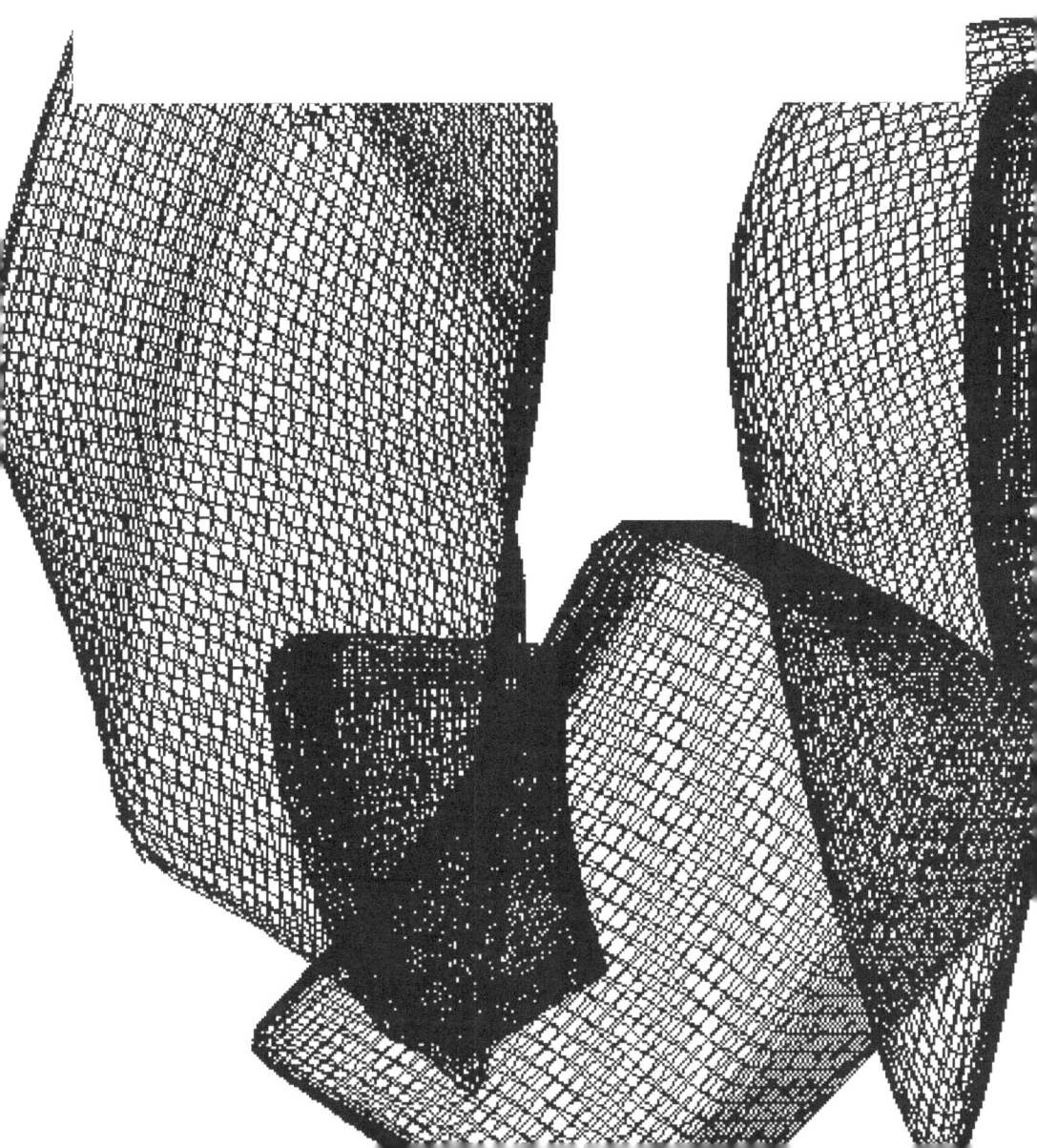

What are your motives?

^

The machine is not rendered inoperable or inaccessible through the obfuscation of its toolset. It is instead made abrupt & multi-directional, preparing itself to function in places both anticipated and not.

^

Its autonomy does not limit the ways that the textobject might be used.

^

In the same turn, the CLOAK does not select its user, it instead attempts to assemble itself in participation with any potential READER / VIEWER.

^

The CLOAK articulates an interface which can be engaged with from every point along its surface.

^

The point of entry can be intended (an incision) or unintended (a tear) and both arrive at the same interior.

^

We look at the same tables of cells. We scry the same organs.

^

Flattening these complex structures into inkblotches along the surface, "I have not abandoned my 2d roots."

^

The CLOAK is contorted and ultimately forms to the shape of the object it is draped over.

This shape hardening into a shell.

^

—we trigger an ecdysis of the outer coating.

^

The textobject unveiling a sensitive new film—something that will harden into the next generation of its CLOAK (cloaking mechanism).

^

Through the semi-translucent skin, there is the silhouette of its organ system.

^

Interconnecting structures (interior design).

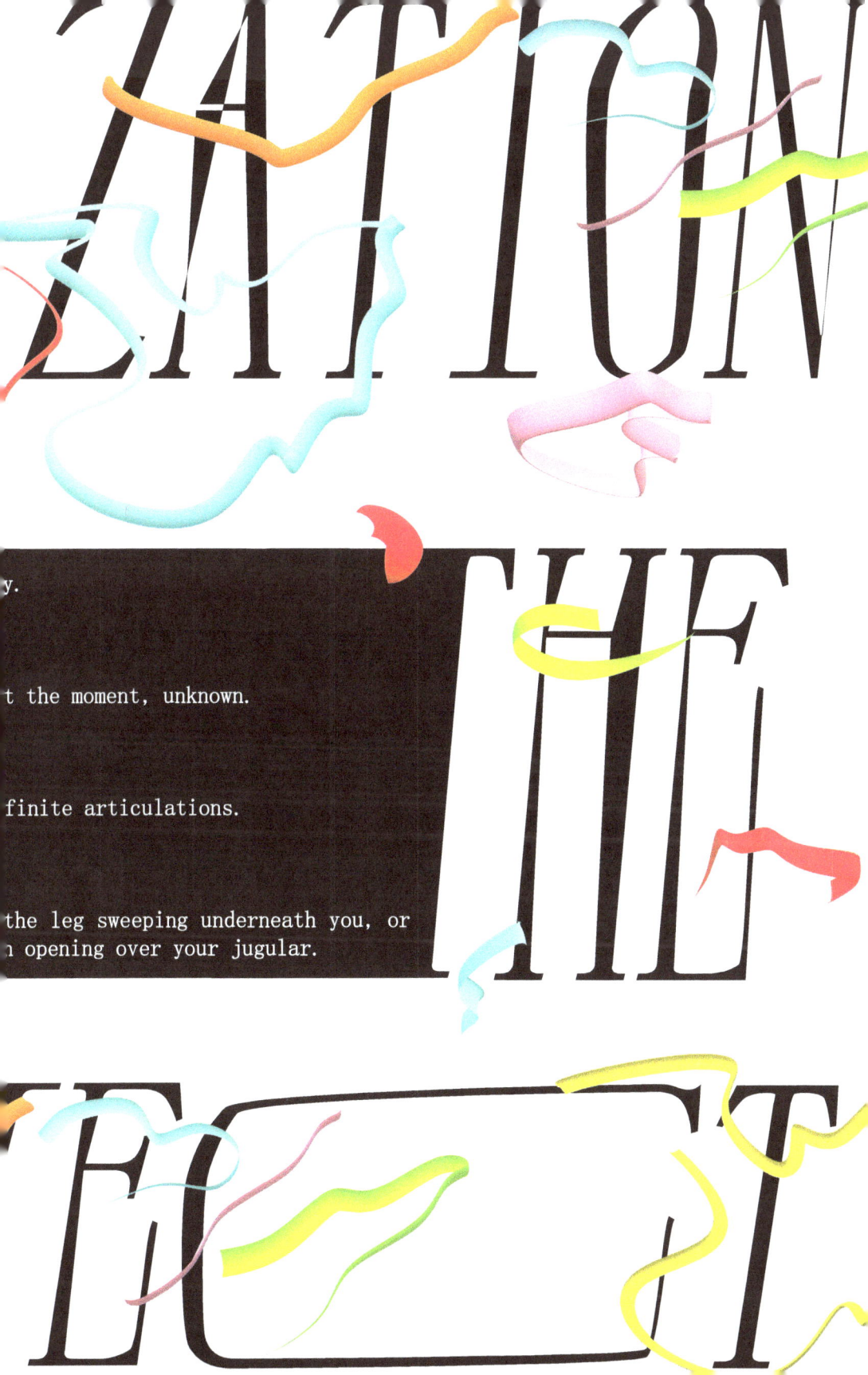

CLOAK V1 — 2022

www.ingramcontent.com/pod-product-compliance
Lightning Source LLC
Chambersburg PA
CBHW072023290426
44109CB00018B/2330